MAYWOOD PUBLIC LIBRARY

12-14-05

# Dark Legs and Silk Kisses

P9-APE-098

Maywood Public Library
121 S. 5th Ave.
Maywood, IL 60153

# DARK LEGS AND SILK KISSES

## THE BEATITUDES OF THE SPINNERS

## ANGELA JACKSON

TRIQUARTERLY BOOKS
NORTHWESTERN UNIVERSITY PRESS
EVANSTON, ILLINOIS

TriQuarterly Books
Northwestern University Press
Evanston, Illinois 60208-4210

Copyright © 1993 by Angela Jackson
Published 1993 by TriQuarterly Books/Northwestern University Press
All rights reserved
Printed in the United States of America
Second paperbound printing 1995

**Library of Congress Cataloging-in-Publication Data**

Jackson, Angela, 1951–

    Dark legs and silk kisses : the beatitudes of the spinners /
    Angela Jackson.

        p.      cm.

    "TriQuarterly books."

    ISBN 0-8101-5026-3 — ISBN 0-8101-5001-8 (pbk.)

    1. Afro-American women—Poetry.    2. Spiders—Poetry.  I. Title.

PS3560.A179D37  1993

811'.54—dc20                        93-26482

                                           CIP

The paper used in this publication meets the minimum requirements of the
American National Standard for Information Sciences—Permanence of
Paper for Printed Library Materials, ANSI Z39.48-1984.

*For my six sisters:*

*Delores, Rosemary, Sharon, Betty Jean, Debra, and Margaret*

*And my sisters-in-law:*

*Leslie and Cynthia*

# Contents

# Acknowledgments

These poems have come to life over the course of nearly a decade. Necessarily, there are many people who have urged, inspired, and responded, to whom I give gratitude, appreciation, and regard: Odette Myers, whose invaluable translation from the French *Book of Symbols* made so many of these poems possible; Sandra Jackson-Opoku and Kofi Opoku, who revitalized Anansi stories with wit and invention; Eleanor Bender, who uncovered the spider poems, and Betty Jean Jackson, DFaye Anderson, and the actors who placed the spiders centerstage; Joyce Carol Thomas, Dr. Carl Djerassi, and the Djerassi Foundation of Woodside, California, where many early poems were born; the OBAC Writers Workshop, and a purpose to drive a lifetime; Leslie Adrienne Miller, for her research for "Tarantula Revolts against the Gravedigging Wasp," and her early audience; Mrs. A., who enables; Susan Hahn, editor with a poet-woman's eye; and especially to Reginald Gibbons, poet, editor, and friend who remembers my work.

I am grateful to the editors of the following journals in which some of these poems appeared: *Open Places*, "Spider Divine," portions of "The Race of Memory," "The Itsy-Bitsy Spider Climbs and Analyzes," "In Her Solitude: The Inca Divining Spider," "The Spider Speaks on the Need for Solidarity"; *Black American Literature Forum*, "The War Chant of the Architect," "Fannie"; *13th Moon*, "Arachnia: Her Side of the Story"; *TriQuarterly*, "Miz Rosa Rides the Bus"; *Steppingstones*, portions of "The Race of Memory"; *NOMMO*, "In Her Solitude: The Inca Divining Spider," "Arachnia: Her Side of the Story"; *River Styx*, "Transformable Prophecy," "RockandRoll Monster: Down Home Blues Goes Hollywood"; *Emergence*, "The Problem in the Closet."

# Lily Looking for a Redcap

There was a time
I would have traveled light.
Climbed down a ladder
with nothing but night
on my back.

And considered myself
lucky
to carry everything I needed
between my legs.

I've got baggage now.

# Journal Entry: August 31, 1983

The other night I discovered a large, gray spider scurrying in the bathroom. Spiders, according to my mother, are a sign of good luck. But this one was a *large* spider; I wasn't sure I would survive its luck. When I smashed her delicate appendages and fuzzy body, I imagined glass breaking. Mirrors.

Later that same evening, a cricket squatted under my coffee table. I eyed it suspiciously. I wondered what a cricket was a sign of. Mama never mentioned crickets, but for some reason I associate them with silence and spaces cushioned with grass. I am accustomed to the sound of collective cricket festivities. A single cricket in your living room is a dumb, ugly creature. I was repulsed by it, but my mood for murder had passed. I let Jiminy live. He leaped across the room and disappeared.

It was the unending and unbearable heat, I thought, that had driven the many-legged creatures inside. They had retreated from the hot cement, the parched and sunbaked lawns, and the thirsty ivy that clung to my house.

The rain came the next day, after weeks of earth-shriveling, stunning, and debilitating heat. In late afternoon, I whistled while I walked through the sprinkle. I thought of the spider and the cricket, and of the wisdom of Nature. In the cloudy ambience of the drizzle, it became clear to me what the spider and the cricket must have known. Surely, Nature had spoken to them, saying, "The drowning, cleansing, and soothing rain is on its way. Go inside and wait."

I know now that I was wrong to kill that spider, even though I feared she would crawl into my bed with me. Poor thing, my sister, she was only following instructions.

# Transformable Prophecy

When the world ends
a great spider will rise like a gray cloud
above it.
She will rise and swell, rise and swell
until she covers green earth, brown rock,
and blue water.
She will seize Creation inside herself
when the world ends
in the last days between the fire and the cold
the ones left will gather tins to beat into shelter
and weeds to eat with decaying mouths
like women in South African bantustans.
They will love what they have gathered among ghosts
and heaped into a place.
The coffee can over smouldering ashes
will hold stone soup.
A thousand species of decay will be born
when the Great Spider squats Creation
back down. A thousand demispecies of spiders
will flourish like flowers walking through
the burning ash, the hot, hot dust.
Crickets will break out of their cages
and tremble down the sky like rain,
twitching on the ground, while the sky turns cold.
The ones left will gather sick skin around bones,
sit in fires that smolder in the earth.
Myriad-legged creatures will scramble through
scorching dust,
legs on fire writing writing prayers God knew
when earth first smoldered, squalled
and begged to be born.

# The Spider Speaks on the Need for Solidarity

*Joyce*

I ain gon lie, she said,
            twining her black legs
            to the velvet of thigh.
I've wanted to murder
a man before.   To walk
over his shut eyes and make
them swell:  blind, infected.

Call it,
        malice.
Call it,
        malevolence.
Call a spade-spider a
spade.
I ain't afraid
of names.
I have always been mis-
understood.

Among Arabs I slip
through purdah.    I do
a mean belly dance
and bodies fall.     Sleeping
dogs lie
forever.

The White Spider, they can love
and call her holy.  She
concealed a prophet
refugee in a cave.  They say.
Slung her long-haired web
across the cave mouth, and
the hunters thought
only bones lay silent inside
instead of a prophet
who could talk.

White spiders they got a thing for her.
A bad case of the hots.    They don't raise
they leg to her.
They don't lift they foot
to walk on her.

They let her be white,
disappearing, a scrambling,
      scampering moon.

They all cringe from the dark ones.
The dark beauty they shun.
I have heard them whispering
down the centuries.

I don't run from nothing.
I just sit
on my own last nerve
and watch,
and wait and plot.

Sometimes I dream spiderly dreams,
magic comes from up

my sleeve
and I swing on magic and weave
my own lullaby
in the amorous air.

I dream of my self,
Black, leaf-fuzzy, fast.

I bless my
spider sisters
in their dark.

We have to weave
one web, a thousand-ark.

We have to stick
together.

# Arachnia:  Her Side of the Story

*Janet*

What Athena weaves best is
lies.      Her and her whole
Olympus family.      Wolfpack of
liars.

She said she was my teacher.
And I swollen imitator, ungrateful
student.
You believe that one?

My body is a busy dark flower
from the dark continent
her Daddy ran-
sacked.    Plundered my pots,
my libraries, my stars,  my
gods.

I wasn't from Lydia
either.  Wrong girl's name.
I'm the dusky girl from
Memphis.

What Athena weaves best is
lies.  Propaganda issued from Olympus.
A thread of deception.
Her stuff sticks to the history
books.
You believe that one?

I wove the real story.
I only embroidered the
                    Truth.
Made it shinier
and it could be seen.
She embroidered seamy press releases
for the Wolfpack
that sits high on the mountain.

She called me blasphemer.
Perjurer.    She slapped me
until I spun.     She says she
sent me to the corner and I
hanged my self.
You believe that one?
That she cursed me and would not let
me die?

     It was a lynch-
rope, my Grecian girl wove
for me.
     It was a lynch-
rope, she spun and lay
and waited for me in a
spooky house.

Wolves bayed in the distance
but I didn't listen.
I was busy looking at the sun
god out of a dirty window
weaving his tapestry.
When she fell on me.

It was my murder.
But not my death.

You see this web?

You ever seen anything like it
in this haunted-house world?

I am still working my charms,
                    quietly.

# The Special Spider

*To Patricia J.*

I have been groomed, you see.
To love all spiders, except for me.
To write the history of the species
by starlight.
I was never taught to fight.

When I considered love
I thought always of a Dark Spider Knight.
No one else could handle my bright
expectations.

Alas, my life is not reparations
for a race.
Once, I was charmed by a silverfish.
Ugly even to me, he was not my dream or my wish.
The only thing that looked like love in this forsaken
place.
He was by no means pretty.
He had a way of seeming kind and witty.
It was only charm.
The reach of his arm
not long enough for me.

Now, solitary, I consider my blight,
how to fight my fate to be apart.
It is simple what I want: the right
to be special to especially me
and someone astride a girder, winking,

while he waves from afar,

Or, he, erudite, and lean
studying the meter of history.

Or, he, flamboyant, and cool
Or, languid in the workless line,
threading diamonds in his spare time.
Or, he, shoulders like a prizefighter
circling, circling, circling in his ring.

Is it wise, do you suppose, to hang in windows,
waiting, when I have work to do
for which I was groomed,
especially?
Today
chores bore me.  Even brilliant.
I languish like any wish pressed against
a windowpane.

# Empty Parlor Blues

*Sarah*

Come into my parlor, said the spider to the fly.
Come into my parlor, said the spider to the fly.
Been so long without you, I think I'm 'bout to die.

Love is like that: it's either me or you.
I said love is like that: it's either me or you.
You think it's me, baby, you're the one who's through.

I made the bed for you to crawl inside.
You know, I was the one made the bed to lie inside.
Now, look at me, I'm caught, nowhere to run or hide.

Come into my parlor, said the spider to the fly.
Come into my parlor, said the spider to the fly.
Been so long without you, I think I'm 'bout to die.

I wish I could, but you know I can't cut you loose.
I wish I could, but you know I can't cut you loose.
I thought I had you, Sugar, I was making my own noose.

Come into my parlor, said the spider to the fly.
Come into my parlor, said the spider to the fly.
I'm so hungry for your loving, baby, I'm 'bout to die.

# Prophet of the Ark

We are the last lovers of land who look out
over waters in search.
First to saunter up the gangplank we touched each other.
Two of a kind.
If there is nothing left I have him to hold
when sky and water are dark and our work
winks in the edges of an ark.
I long for earth, a trapdoor, for cave, in which to hide
a bell.
But nothing is born here; we maintain
till land is in our sight and all begin to multiply.
Embracing. Coupling. In amazement at this
miracle. This God who is able
when we are lost children of many species,
thirsting for ground, for branch, for dry luck.

# Reflection on College Avenue, Columbia, Missouri

Hanging in midair the web is a batik of sunlight and air,
a thin chalk drawing scribbled on the wind.
And wind is kind to it; leaves it a name in ancient saliva
that anyone literate in this language can read, the hieroglyphics
of a life this side of the river, details in a week's worth of
weaving, in a voice shrill and exquisite like a market woman's,
a natural grafitti, clandestine and superb in incandescent tongues
a convex collection of vigilante moonbeams turning to sun.
What ancestral sarcophagus has come unwrapped in this american
autumn where refugee birds tunnel through air and quit this
disquiet place before some loping lie swallows them whole?
What serenity does sister-weaver know who spun off from the
stippled sign of the adult education center to batik her name and
mine like a confident prayer on the wind? How has she done this?
How can this be, but
From the ground up.
To the middle branch of the ash tree.
Leaving a silver banister for me.

# Spinster Song: African-American Woman Guild

*for Ginger*

We'll all be Penelopes then.
Weaving by day, untying by night.
Deceiving the lovers who are not
quite right.

Waiting for heroes' arrival from fields
unraveling with bloody arts.
Throwing aside their cool shining shields
that cover their breakable hearts.

It's wasteful to be Penelope.
Spending days doing nothing
to undo nights.
Lying about loving
or knots.

I'd rather be in fields
Stripping away shields
Aiming needles at suitable
hearts.

# The Silk Sisters

*for my six sisters*

One mother emptied us from her body like teardrops
she laid us on a sheet of silk
and spread warm semen over us.
Till the ones who would live chose living.
She rolled us together in a sac
and carried us on her back
or hung us from a cave roof
in an elegant bell.

We breathed each other's silence
for a good time.

Each breath an echo bent back
and sent out again.

Each body a sister planet
in a cozy, swaying galaxy.

Wandering far
we have never been lost.

There is no betrayal of the original bell.

We have never been lost.

# Why the Dark Ones Tremble

The dark ones are easy to pluck.
Like a flower in a game of whimsy.
She loves me.  She loves me not.
She loves me.
You cannot deny the dark is delicious.
But nothing worth keeping, so
you are careless.
Poor creature crawling up a man's arm
close to him and closer.
Do you see her dark, formidable and fragile?
The pain you inflict on her
is the pain you feel inside
being dark as she
and who you are denied
because the dark is dazzling to behold
and must be subdued with curses
and eyes that look upon us cold.

# Billie in Silk

I have nothing to say to you, Billie Holiday.
You do not look at me when I try to speak to you.
You cannot look me in the eye.  Your eyes
look elsewhere.
Your steamy mouth sewn up with red tears
is poised to speak
to someone.
The orchid in your hair grows, grows like
a spider turning herself inside out.
The shadow hangs
into your eye.

I have smiled the way you
do not smile.
I was just out of love,
and cold.
I was naked, beyond caring.
My smile, like yours, was a wry line
beside my steamy mouth.
My eyes, like yours, didn't look at me,
I only saw the fall
from
grace.

       (You lay down with music in the leaves.
       You wrapped him in leaves, in sheets.
       Your legs lindyed around him.  Young
       then old.  Do not be deceived.  The
       thunder of the spider is no small
       thing.  You had your way with music,

and ate him.  The memory hot
in your belly.  Ours.)

*You never want to let her leave.*
*She.  The voice deceives.*
*You could hurt it.*
*It would kill you*
*too.*
*The dragline seeking*
*curving above Surprise.*
*Below*
*Just so.*
*Size is not the issue.*
*Volume not*
*the question.  A hairline*
*fracture in the Silence*
*in which nothing rests.*
*The voice deceives.*
*Every thing*
*swings.*

I have something to say to you, Billie Holiday.
Sew up your breathing, then send it back to me.
Fluent and ruminating the source of such anguish.

Look into my eyes.

If only it were not so lonely to be black and bruised
by an early-morning dream
that lifts the mouth to sing.

Here is an orchid, spideresque-petaled, glorious,
full of grace.

My mouth is on fire.  Let it burn.

# In Her Solitude: The Inca Divining Spider

*Ana*

It is dark in the pot
where he keeps me.   The Inca priest
with gold rings on his golden wrist.
El Dorado.   I smell the clay and the sweat
from the human hands that made
my bowl of solitude.
Where I wait in darkness,
captive, humming.

The priest, his hand trembles when he
lets in sun to look at me.
He squints
at the way I sit.
When I sprawl, legs spread,
extravagantly, loitering
in my pot—it's a good sign
and his teeth glint a smile.
When I sit
with even one leg folded
under me
like the woman that I am
with a bad attitude—he trembles
from smile to fingers—
tremors.   I am a Bad
Omen.

He seals me in again

and prays and prays
for my legs to
open.

# Work: African-American Woman Guild

*of Soyini*

A fury in her as she weaves.
Legs factory-fast.  Assembly lines /  laundromat spins /
A blurry tumble /  acute activity.   Spinnerets
 nets nests / cocoon /  web-trap.


Ah, the fierce, fine fiber / nests, cocoons, en-
traps.      Enraptures in leg-pits.
She names her work
so:
designed digit-prints

spun,
swung,
earth to sky /  birth to die /
back again she loops,
eightlegged,   industrious /  rapid-reverent /
furious!
her vertiginous /
rise /
streamlined /  integral /
wise.

# Love:  African-American Woman Guild

*for Jacqui*

There is a certain /

                              way to hold /

            with / so many legs

                  she / has

                        to

                        learn:


            be quick /

                              light /

                  persist.


Not too pushy
like an ant /


                        Not to grab
                        prey like a man-
                        tis. /

But swiftseize
or studiedmagnificent
weave—

                        expert /

                                    superb /

                        she learns

her entire /  life
is spinning /

                        trying to hold
                        and keep her
                        self in.

# Conjugal Bed: African-American Woman Guild

*for Christine*

A married man is a spider-
mummy, wrapped in gossamer, gauze
guilt.  Necessity.  Seduced, secured, silenced
                        with spidery
                            kisses.

# Fannie (of Fannie Lou Hamer)

Fannie sang in jailhouse cells.
Don't you know her songs
swung the bars
high in the window
back and forth between snot
hard tears and stars.

Fannie Hamer sang about climbing
Jacob's ladder

                    rung
                    by
                    rung
that cottony voice rose
                    above smoke
and robes and swamps, dust
roads, lynch ropes, and water
hoses, dogs, badges, and mud
weary beaten bones and bullets.

Miz Fannie sang about climbing
Jacob's ladder, wrestling
angels, climbing

swinging rung by rung, from crying
                              to shining
bringing one by one,      from crying
                              to shining
          as far as the heart can
          see,
          as far as the back can
          carry.

Fannie sang in jailhouse cells.
Don't you know her songs?

Have you ever seen a Queen Spider dance?
She seems to be kneeling, but is not.
She is always getting up.

Have you ever seen a Queen     Spider dance?
Some of them have wings.

# I Sit and Sew

Worn down, exhausted. Unslept.
Weary of empty blame dispensed
to men who would blame me
for their crimes. I took to bed
and began a plan.

Since then, a habit of mine to sew.
grew.
And so I do.
This private labor
entrance to a greater rage.
Meticulous, directed as the needle
I stick in cloth and take it out again.
Clean. I dream of voodoo
as I stick in my pin.

These are the eyes.
This is the heart.
The legs cannot run away.
The heart is empty anyhow.

I see figures fainting in my material.
I see dead bodies.
On his knees, anyone I please.
Imagine such ruin, imagine such righteous rendering
of penance.
There is no mercy in my needle.
Only a justice serene and clean
upon which I sit and sew.
And now and then I prick my own finger

and draw a drop of blood
because the malice that won them
the point of my needle injured someone
sweet on me who had no recompense
but this keen voodoo or a keening, unkempt,
unvindicated.

What a wonderful war is mine
the way I even things out in time.
Sewing.

# Her Beatitude

*for Brandi*

Hallowed be the little one.
Whose work is never done.

Blessed be the poor
given little who makes it
more
inside herself
"interior liberty"
a wealth
of beatitudes.

Blessed be the prayers
and sacrifices she hangs
upon her lines.
May sunlight strike
them visible.
May we be no longer
blind
to her needs.

Hosanna to her enduring
when wind is hurricane.
Shakes the pedestals
on which her hope leans
rises and wanes.

Glory be to she
who plucks the garden clean

from pests.
So that our fruits
fatten and yield.

Praise her.
Praise her.

# Black Widow

*in memory of my grandmothers*

The sons come home again
to sit around her, reworking
their lives as they fidget in them
starched and itchy.

Her daughters scurry,
bringing her kin, "See. Don't she,
Don't he, look like so-and-so?"

    The roads that bend
before her house, all the ways to go
one place, or another.
A husband is dust,
rough-sliding through knotted fingers.
Her hands gave up:  she gave up the Singer.
Her fingers turned cold:  she turned in the quilting.

A day is scattered in thought.
Night is one slow walk
through an old house.
In the dark she knows
where everything is.
      Two stiff legs,
two stiff arms, the four-legged silver
walker.
Eight limbs tell her
it's late.

Imagine all the pieces she can put together
when she takes up quilting again.

This square minute next to this round moment.
Ubiquitous seconds.
Nothing but time on her hands.

# The Problem in the Closet

*of the brown recluse, for Tom and Judith*

Her problem is theological.
She sits in the closet and broods.
The door is shut.
She moves under the tongue of a shoe.
Can't figure it out, sole and tongue,
The things we hold on to.

Heaven is a shelf she can't reach.
And the dimwit sun is never on.
She keeps going to the far corner,
the darkest spot.  The forgivable shadows know
what she doesn't.

All that darkness and a sole to subdue.
That should be enough.
Her mind wanders on someone.
"I don't feel sorry for you.
I don't feel sorry for you
at all."

A cause for gall.

"Just you wait."  She eyes the shelf
Still, under the tongue.
"Just you wait." Fidgets, she wants to settle
a debt.
Seven times seven.

She can't figure it.
The things we hold on to, the molded shirt,
the sleeve with the hole she burned through.
It was supposed to be sweet.

But it's sour.  How do you sort it?
What thing we reach for in the dark,
then run up on this bit of living
Spite.

## Dementia Dexter

When I open my arms to you, Friend,
It is because Dementia loves
Company.
Here.  Be comfortable.
Let me pour you eye-wine.
Please, don't tell me your problems.
I have poisons of my own.  See?
I said, "See."
And don't see anything else.
Until I tell you to.
My injury is superior.
You must bow.
Like that.
Yes. Like that.

Oh, how I love you, Friend.
I could eat you up!

# ALYO

*for Muntu*

We have to speak to your Death.
We have to say something
          to the trouble in your lungs.
We have to say that trouble does not win.
We have to see you lifting your body
    legs-spread in a spidery African leap.
We have to remember how you denounced
    gravity.
We have to hold the sun in your eyes
      as you who never grimaced,
      who was masked, resplendent with sun.
We have to keep your sweat alive
      on your face while you spider-danced
      under lights
      a white handkerchief in your hand
      drenched with salt.
We have to speak to the quiescent spirit
      who was shy in you
      who loitered like a boy in the vestibule of our
applause.
We have to say something
      about the Love      dancing in a coat of straw
                      trembling,  troubled by air
      on fire with
      the Lights.

How you leapt      lifting us high, quick and strict.
All of the good things in your limbs.

# The Spider Tells Her Horror Stories

I have my horror
stories.  If you are a seeker
of thrills or guilt, I'll tell
them to you.  I hate them heavy
in my mouth.  Hovering.  I keep
them out
or quiet.  But

my body is tremulous
                    fiber-swollen
threatens breaking out—
pouring a silken pouch of horror
stories wild scramble
directionless, dangerous,
unguided.

                    A life ago I gave up
                    the wearisome, winding whine.
                    I haven't missed her
                    since.  She was never cunning-
                    mine.  Some stray strand;
                    pitiful outsider
                    who wandered into a nest
                    of spiders.

Even I
have no sufficient howl.
Not enough thunder
in the cups of my eyes

to slit irises, let out
the barren spaces, the
beseiged lives.

Even I
who have multiple eyes
enough to see and cry
at the same time
for boys on the corners
            like lampposts flickering
         spirits scattered into shattered
         lights.
Even I
have my ghosts.

Quick, out of my mouth!
Spider-ghosts.

Who was elephant-gunned down at 16 who was
pregnant for the second time.  Gunned down
before her daughter's eyes who was two.
Baby-faced and sweet, who modeled black
in a fashion show, who was gone

who was my best friend once whose 17-year
breath was pressed back into her until she
drowned by her husband's hand husband who
held the breath of a woman before her until
her heart stopped stupid loving, and her eyes
emptied out

"Her boyfriend cut her up.
Talkin about if he can't have her
nobody else can."

Darling,
I will give you
horror.

who was pretty and yellow
with black-sea soft hair,
she would not have him.
      He ————————————————

Did I tell you this
story before?

Did you cry?

And with how many eyes?

Aren't you tired of horror
stories?  Of lonely terror
looking lopsided into a whiskey glass.
Of wet sorrow growing
in the corners of eyes.

Of my belly full of horror stories
that scramble toward the mike
to be heard?

Silence these wandering witches then.
Stirring up their trouble in your delicate
mind.   Shut them up
with lush lullabies.
Make my brutish tales
lumbering lies.
Obsolete.  Extinct.
Fossils and dead charms.

Rest the ghosts.

If you are a seeker of love,
come to Anansi-daughter.

I have graceful, grateful arms
as my sisters do.

We embrace you with our eyes.

We see you, lover,
as you stretch with a web in your palm.

Held so tender
it does not break.

# Sexual Harassment

*for Theresa*

He thinks you
are a flower
and cannot talk.
So still standing
there.
Touching no one
In your splendid garb.
You are free.  Must be.
So many parts to you
belonging to you.
Invite him.
When he takes his scissors,
his eye sly,
he aims to sever a stalk.
How could he know you would bleed?
And he would be to blame
and find a lie
to hide behind.  Make it wide.
A rock behind which to hide his face.
With so many spiders underneath.
Crawling out from under.

*Being I, arachnid-splendored, with mouth.*
*This story feeds me like flies.*

# Art: African-American Woman Guild, or The Spider Explains Her Art to the Blind

*for Sheron*

When I have fine-tuned my scream
into glinting swords crisscrossing where I have cursed.

When I have smashed nightmares and walked them like thin,
flat pearls; danced their spines like a buckdancing ballerina.

When I have cradled out into night like a star
unwinding itself; unspooling devils who dim-ride my light.

When I have reached out my beam in the doorway,
pulling out my heart muscle in endless scarves of rain-
bowing songs, and carry each one in to meet my source.

In stormy weather
I send my leg out through a slit
and turn round under thunder
I craft my moves from loas' moods
work the back like Oshun do when she do
Damballah groove in the mudrunning earth.

When I twirl my baton like an axis in earth-circles
too quick for the eye.

When I dip my pen in a well of dark tears and write
with a flourish my signature song, a fancy agony, my painted
ache.

When I am big enough to stretch the lion's jaws between
thumb and index finger; when I sit inside his mouth
all night.

When I dance like strokes of fire above blind heads.

When I am strange wind opening doors.

When I blow my silent silver bell above the river
and kneel in it without breaking.

When I perform my feats
who sees?

When I stretch miracles
they are miracle blind.

When I dance pins
they applaud devils.

When I level screams with bladed ends
they assume I plea.

They don't know me or my family.
I am from the line of Oshun,
Anansi's kinswoman,
Damballah daughter.

I am the singer with no name
fine-tuning screams to grace that keens
crisscrossing in the sky.

I am the cradling star stripping devils before morning.

I am an angel dancing on the head of a pin.
No one can count these steps.

I am spinning earth's axis.

I am lotus sitting in the lion's mouth.

I am breathing in a silver bell.

I am beaming in the doorway.
Either come inside or
Get out of my light.

# Sweatshop of the Singing Hosts

*for Sandra and Adjoa; Kofi and Kadallah*

A host of spiders weave inside her.
They close their copious eyes like women
singing soaring notes.

Blind, blessed, believing in becoming
flesh, sinew-spiel: substance.
They make the bone to the bone they walk the bone
as they go      carefully on cartilage.

They know as they go
balancing
marrow, and magic.

When she is pregnant as roundly now
she is always doing two things.
Being two beings.

              She sits swollen at her table
              writing poems,

                      and the Other.
              She washes dishes and does
                     the Other.
              She turns clumsily in the bed
              beside her husband, and beds
                  another.
              She vomits all she has taken in-
              side herself, and holds

                    something in.

In these gossamer-glowing days, her body separate and
vibrant,
If she placed her latticed palm across her belly
she would know the time of seamstresses sweating
sewing
            around the quiet, tiny, ticking clock.

# The War Chant of the Architect

*Toni Cade Bambara*

I am the architect of the bridge in the music:
Seven horns soloing silver stepping stones walking
One horn echoing gold in a steady drumbeat.

> I built the bridge over bone-crushing
> river. I did not look down in flight.
> Drylongso like always, unassuming just
> believing in the boomerang of giving.
> You can call that holy if you want.
> I call it working.

I am the alchemist stirring in the heat in the heart:
out of blues I spin gold.
Crafty Anansi-daughter outwitting Rumpelstiltskin
in this day
in this time.

Once
I stole fire from the lions, because it was
mine.
I sold the Sky God's words to the trees.
I sat among naked birds and wove them
wings.

Oh, I cry out of soiled monotony counting steps
in tenements and urine-drenched projects. I scurry
from the Hawk, with two shopping bags weighing me
in the wind.  Overpriced groceries and sold-

stolen dreams leaking out through brown paper seams.
I slip sidewalk cliffs and wise cracks, slanting
mouths pointing down. I tremble in the squalor
of discounted flesh and blood and memory, in squandered

dignity, in refused beauty, in shunted hopes
and locked treasure and lost key.

> I go about my doing. Consuming by-products
> of waste and strange and bitter fruits.
> I call it working. Making doilies for TV
> tops, washing lace and washing weeping
> away Sundays when I sing or sleep late.
> It's all routine, but deep inside I
> dare a dream. Dare a dream.

When I hear the heavy footsteps with heavy soles
and lead heels

When I hear them walking close

I run for cover, calling mother
calling father, uncles, aunts, cousins,
brothers, sisters,
a multitude of my line
to come and drop down
like armies of black rain,
crawling nightmares of the worst kind.
Stroking white machetes in the night.

But I am quiet now, doing what a brown woman does at dusk
and deeper. Braiding my hair and singing old songs
rising on the spines of trees, sending shivers

through the wind.

I am only remembering the singing memory
Because remembering is fighting.
Remember.

I am the architect of the bridge in the music.
Climbing sheer air over crushing rivers, urine-
drenched projects, dirty tenements, Hawk and hucksters,
hustlers and empties cast aside glinting broken
in moonlight.  Over sneering overseers and war worship
where mostly the dark die, over heavy bootsteps, hair-
maim, neon adoration, dross, notions and nothings sold
over the counter singing endless deprival in my american
dreams.  Climbing sheer air over shuffling, inadequate
mime-men, do-less, dead-eyed lost, playing muscle games
and video, fist-in-the-face desire, slash and burn
tenderness where nothing blooms in soil no deeper
than a TV screen.

I am braiding my hair and singing old songs while dark
walks in  from the window and trees make bridges in the
slow wind while things unseen go about their drylongso,
I sing old songs and remember who

I am the alchemist making blues gold.
African daughter outwitting gnome.
I stole my fire from the cold lions.
I sold wisdom to trees.
I sat naked among naked birds and wove
them wings.

# Totem: African-American Woman Guild

*Artists for Harold Washington*

In the middle of the day, the world
alive in the house.
A spider
bobbing delicately down from kitchen ceiling
on a lean single
thread—a sign
Mama said
of a guest coming,
someone you haven't seen
in a long time.

You,
dangling from cornerless sky
out of nowhere,
what surprise visitor
is on the way
we haven't seen for a mighty
long time?
Coming down the road singing
victory
in harmony
with us.

Creature of faith,
who climbs down and
up on a single breath
line, who trusts the thread

unbreaking—

I believe I hear someone
coming down the road
singing victory
home at last
among us.

# RockandRoll Monster: Down Home Blues Goes Hollywood

*for 5527 and the television tribe*

She was sitting in her black jook cave
listening to blues, eating bats, and getting fat
when the lightbread people came.
She ate the first man for a snack.

Then the daughter came, with yellow celery down her
back and a boyfriend
and pretty soon a hippy blues spider
can't win.
They took her in,
put her on drugs and propped her in a museum.
Took her blues away.     And she slept,
numb, out of it.
Roped in and stupid.
Captured.
Came alive in a museum in 1957.

Some white kids were playing
rockandroll before the mashed potatoes.
Loud enough to wake the dead or dopey.
Woke the rockandroll in her pitch bush
body.  She got up on the wrong side of
no bed.  Hair standing all over her head.
Catching radio waves.   The Voice of God
she thought it was.  She just wanted to
put her hand on the music box and be saved.
Sounded like somebody she knew from home.

But no—indeed—they snatched the
bumpy tune and fled.  Scattered down main
street with her musical treat.  All she
long for was a good meal after a long sleep.

Evil Gal Blues under her swampy lid.
Crashed
a fine, unshaved leg
through teeny-tiny whitey trim window.
Like a black whip snapping law and order.

Watched the pastel people pee and flee.
Stalked high-heeled blondes with screaming
brussel sprouts in their arms.
All looking good enough to eat, but
rescued in the knick of time.

Monster wanna rockandroll over
in her own bed
back in the jook-joint cave.
She moonwalk her Regal walk on home.
Ate
Sheriff intruder at her leisure.
His whole body
hors d'oeuvres.
His skeleton left
an empty lazy susan.

She just wanna pick her teeth, snap
her fingers, drink a bloody mary, and listen
to some down-home blues. Loud.
She wanna lay around with her hair wild
and legs unstyled.  Smell her own funk
and dream the rest of her cave-black night.

Got.  Instead
A mouth full of dynamite.

Ain't that cold-
blooded?

# The Institutional Spider

What you have whispered to her
when the room was empty of all
but quiet she
has taken and given to a thousand ears.
Her hair is a brush she paints with.
She creates questions about you.
She likes to get even with you
because she cannot make what you
make.

Craftless, save for a malice-mischief
so small it spreads over her good
eye.  She is blind, but knows her
territory so well she can feel
her way around.  Whispers are her
trade.  She is wild
with ambition.  Yet cannot create;
she mimics compassion and begs
it for herself.

If you caught her and cut her open,
there would be a small wound
itching to be fed.  Someone
should sew her up.  Her mouth.

When the light hits she runs
from office to office.
Looking for some place safe
where no one recognizes her
work and loves her bright specks

of movement.  Prettily she schemes
and denies the weeping she leaves
behind her.

When she gloats she swells up
and is big.  No one can catch her.
No one can catch her.

Suddenly, a mirror.  She surveys
another spider.  Lunges.  Falls
back.  Stupid and surprised.
"I thought I was the Only.  I
thought I was the Only Only.
I thought I was the One."
As a sun that meets another sun,
fire collides.  The Only withers
and surely she dies.  What is
born I cannot say.  She took
my secrets you see.  I do not know
the penalty.  I cannot measure
her wound.  I cannot say her
destiny.  What is left is up to her
and her alone.  Alone at last
I cannot name her decent task.

# The Itsy-Bitsy Spider Climbs and Analyzes

*for Nora*

The sadists squeal with glee
in the nursery,
while tiny limbs break.
They chant my peril like soprano
gestapo.  Blonde-banged, spit-polished,
rose-cheeks and toothless tulips.
They sing the bright, evil tune
because their mothers hate me
and teach them rhyming hate.
They have no symphonic sympathy
and tell my story with murderers'
hands.  Hatchet-hands.  Hose hands.
They send me up my wall again.
Bedraggled and futile.  Ligaments-broken.
Eyes-lost.  Limp.

Soon they tire of my agony.

Their mothers teach them new
hand tricks for the heartless:
This is the church.  This is the steeple.
Open the doors and in come the people.

# The Dung Spider

Here she sits
on a hill of shit.
Hers and anybody else's
she can find.
The smell
doesn't bother her.
It is the smell of new wine
in the old bottle of humus.
She'll make something of this
hill of shit.
She'll take tidbits
of your life and screw
them all together.
When she gets through
you won't be you.
Inventive isn't she-it?

I want to bury this bitch
at the bottom of this pile
where the scorpions hide.
But she is worth less
than the stink she sinks
into as she spreads it
around.

She has no mother.
She has no father.
She has no brothers.
She has no sisters.
She was never born.

Was something thought of
to embody a little hate
that will never amount
to much.

# The Aztec Spider:  A Terrible Woman

"If I was eating people
daily sacrificing arenas
amphitheaters of villagers, captured, conquered,
I'd dream a terrible spider
that sought to salt
me and eat
me too."

O, Black Tarantula of conscience
descending like a stormcloud
from the sky.

Even rain turns to
Venom!

# Tarantula Revolts against the Gravedigging Wasp

*for Keoropetse Kgositsile and the Freedom Fighters of
Southern Africa*

I spend my life weaving in three dimensions,
in solitary pursuit of fragile symmetry.
Repetition of changes in my divine monotony.

I do not break my pattern.

I must not trouble my mind with dreams
that do not evolve between my legs.
I know what I know.
Am happy knowing
the ease of thread through eyes,
the breeze on my belly.
Isn't Joy enough
if I own my own service?

Once Joy was enough.

In late summer, when the sun draws cool
silence
against my designs, the blue wasp arrives.
She wanders all over me.
She is Marco Polo visiting China.
She is Perry walking in the black snow of
my hairs.
She is Columbus who has traveled wrong
and found the right island.

She says she knows me
who has never known me
and all that my body offers.
She greets me gratefully.
I welcome her.  I am a gracious host.
I have spent my lives in lonely pursuit
of symmetry.
I have never imagined her.

There is sorcery in the flight
of blue wings.

Then she comes for me.  Blue flame-winged
malice.
I rise to fight.
We bruise dance black and blue as
we tangle.
We roll,
somersault,
tumble together.
She finds my soft spot and shoots me full
of nightmares.  At last,
I lie lost, vanquished.

Dreamily, I watch the blue wasp dig
my grave.
Dreamily, I watch the gravedigger wasp.
I observe my murder.
She drags me to my grave.
She plants her egg on me.

Out of the egg the larva bursts
hungry, at first, minuscule.
It feasts on nectar

from my abdomen.  It devours
my eyes, my genitals.
It colonizes,
consumes.
It grows strong.

Its young body glued to my belly,
tunneling through my underside.

When I am little left
but bones standing dry
its young will be strong
and walk upright;
even fly.

In exile
In secret
In open wise
I blood-weave this message across
this sky—
This is not the natural order of things.

In exile
In secret
In open wise
I draw myself in three dimensions.
I smash the witch-wasp's spell.
I tear her wings into confetti
to cushion
my nest.
I have murder in all my eyes.

Whoever of me dies
dies alive.

# Arachnophobia 1992

In Africa, during drought, when children turned to sticks
cast down into the many names of God,
and all was left to dry,
the people said, "If someone asks you must say Yes."
Yes.

Trust no one now in this place
when everywhere is dying;
the forms of dying travel by night,
hunger beneath daylight.
Bodies wince and spirits recoil in the excruciating twirl.
Trust no one hunched in a territory of beggary, theft, and greed.
Even a little one no longer a sign of peace.
They are everywhere.
The ones who will do you
harm.
Fear the shadow approaching on the sidewalk under lamplight.
He may be the carrier of ignominious end.
Two females, innocent enough?, one of them with child.
Trust no one now. A child is a witness to anything.
Even her own debasement.

Step lightly.
Lightly.

# Sermon of the Middle-Aged Revolutionary Spider

WHEN SPIDER WEBS UNITE, THEY CAN FELL A LION.
—African proverb

*Carole*

There is no inherent evil in ambition.
No error to desire to dream the Revolution, the Spin
that Spins
the Change.
To be a simple spider and dare
against the Lion.

Better to dare in moments, to build
minute by minute minute the death
of injustice, the demise of tyranny,
the surprise attack against
The Lion.
To devote oneself daily to the manufacture
of a trap connected to a thousand
traps, to wrap a lion in, cocoon tight,
to hold him imprisoned in a thousand just and necessary
creations, until the time—released—
he is made new, our brother again.
To build bridges to each other that defy
the destruction in the normal course.
To be bridges, locked upright around
this giant, this lion—There is nothing grandiose
in this dream,
only grandeur.

To cast our nets
in such a way so as to seize sunlight
and light rain and withstand heavy pourings
while gathering every good
deed and promise and binding these
in a word of mercy—We who
have given tender are entitled to be
comforted.

To enjoy the stretch and strength the momentary
luxury of weaving, or after,
or before, the sense of reach and inner
repair, consummated, magnanimous,
the self extended beyond itself into
opalescent streams,
there is a pleasing pleasure in this
art, a joyment, simple and wholesome,
a well-being in which we echo through
to each other, a caveat that is filled,
overflowing with sunlight, dazzling the shine
that touches, to which we
respond—There is a vibration
that sets kindred strands to trembling,
a frequency of longing and repletion;
There is a vibration that causes
us to gather at once, separate and intact,
and seize the Lion, squeezing,
slowly, day against day, night by night,
until we bring him, breathless, to his knees.

Then we will play that vibration
till he rises anew—our brother again.
No longer the tyrant of cruelty and greed,
No longer overwhelmed by his own power.

At last, done with the violence that suspends his heart.
Unburdened from his burdensome deceit.
Shaken loose from his impotent roar;
we will play that vibration, small as we are,
magnificent in victory, grand in ambition,
then we will ride our own work from star to star,
taking as long as it takes us to make bridge, and net and
moral conduit, moment by moment.

# The Cobweb Boat of Columbia Spider

*The Gospel Singers at Joyce's*

I've been to hell and back on a cobweb boat.
I carried lost souls down the river of doom.
        Here I go
        to and fro
    on the stranded vessel
       Such crying!
       Such gnashing of teeth!
    No soul can sever the ties that bind
    them to their ends.

It is too late, I cry.
Too late.

I am a just woman, sailor for a just God:
        cold-blooded; with many eyes
         all justly
         blind.
      A face turned away.

Mercy weeps on the banks amidst the mud of life.

It is too late.   Mercy erodes and slides and flows
down the river of despair.   Fierce trees shiver at
my passing.

I sail now, deaf and deft;
a thousand wails trapped in a cobweb canoe.

I couldn't hear nobody pray, even if I wanted to.

## Scientists Gave a Group of Spiders LSD and Watched Them While They Wove Aberrant, against the Patterns of Nature

a drug trip /
          they sent me
/ my luggage half-
        packed
   spilling
   behind me /
        these streets
crooked /   very very wonder
a drive-by /   mission
       a joyride
       behind me /
           these streets
       seeping
       broken milk bottle /
           heads
       leaking brain /
          a splash
       a heat brand steaming /   yo!  in concrete
        behind me /
          these streets
remember.  if i could
remember (sunlight breaks
distorts /
haunted) remember
who it was i /   never knew
but crashed /   crooked

across the evening
news no one wants to have

whatchu
whatchu expect
? we dancing specks and attitudes
bump into
the streets
draw blood
in the hood
who
screaming
? who
screaming
inside me
            leaking /
                        these streets
not
            by nature
            by rope to—

by bogus. Juice.

# Miz Rosa Rides the Bus

That day in December I sat down
by Miss Muffet of Montgomery.
I was myriad-weary.  Feet swole
from sewing seams on a filthy fabric;
tired-sore a-pedalin' the rusty Singer;

dingy cotton thread jammed in the eye.
All lifelong I'd slide through century-reams
loathsome with tears.  Dreaming my own
silk-self.

It was not like they all say.  Miss Liberty Muffet
she didn't
jump at the sight of me.
Not exactly.
They hauled me
away—a thousand kicking legs pinned down.

The rest of me I tell you—a cloud
Beautiful trouble on the dead December
horizon.  Come to sit in judgment.

How many miles as the Jim Crow flies?
Over oceans and some. I rumbled.
They couldn't hold me down. Long.
No.

My feet were tired.  My eyes were
sore.  My heart was raw from hemming
dirty edges of Miss L. Muffet's garment.

I rode again.

A thousand bloody miles after the Crow flies
that day in December long remembered when I sat down
beside Miss Muffet of Montgomery.
I said—like the joke say—What's in the bowl, Thief?
I said—That's your curse.
I said—This my way.
She slipped her frock, disembarked,
settled in the suburbs, deaf, mute, lewd and blind.
The bowl she left behind. The empty bowl mine.
The spoiled dress.

Jim Crow dies and ravens come with crumbs.
They say—Eat and be satisfied.
I fast and pray and ride.

# The Race of Memory

*for Soyini*

I collect the race of memory, even in my stance, quiet, octave quiet. Not even one thread will quiver, no bough of silver break, no cradle, no lattice lullaby, no heart's sweet arc gives way, no despair too heavy to hang lulling without dying only sleeping sorrow in a suspended animation of prayer. Even as I feign sleep in an old dream history plays past my eyes and I step in line amble up the plank with my husband at my side and he paces the deck for forty watery days and watery nights while I etch a tapestry a prophecy of doves and olive branches just what god told me and bent it all inside a rainbow even though they all called me crazy and I took my hurt and wove that too in a blanket-drawing good as new until that boat ride ended in a promise that came true because I had already drawn it down. But then the ride that broke my heart, pressed my legs so tight beside my kinswomen none of us would write a reason for such agony, aimlessly we twisted making no prints in the heavy heaving lightlessness in a passage in the middle of hell from one end to another knowing not even the one beside me or her language the thinking thoughts flew back at me from my dry, gritty mouth and lacerated my face in scarifications and scars not my art or my doing only desperate response then amid the heavy heaving rocking I learned the work of memory and remembering turned the old ways into my deep brain and deep muscle and commissioned it to stay and come out like light every now and then and guide me.

Now I take my dizzying labyrinth and watch it lead me to Africa again, O mostly the men weave there. Sit cross-legged at their handlooms, cutting sunlight with their teeth of the gap-toothed smile. Fingers crossing sunrise with blue night, spin yarns and yarns through blue dye that does not die. Far across the broken rivers of the cloth, through the tangled language threads where we lie tongue-tied beside each other:

bowels        house dismembered        names scattered I gathered nimble craft and graced the mother's braid that names the names of kinswomen   clothlooming men on this girl-drop of my own spit a halo hosanna!  What more could I have done beyond memory that protects, a nimbus of nimble-digit story to carry to the crossroads of hue, sex, and aristoi where I fidget and get on with it, in the ceaseless legwork of the detective-destiny who brings all to justice.  Spit on the iron and spit sizzles, disappears like days spent spitting and spinning at some other's wheel of profit.  Trading stories like silk along the line where many legs cramp and spit dries to ennui, spite, and blunt grief.  They called the women workers spiders in the cloth factories. Acknowledging this guild, this mystery. Now who is webster for Poly Ester and wants to tell it? At the crossroads of gender, hue, and aristoi my myth sits in someone else's pocketbook pulling fortune after me while sisters wish and call my name repeatedly like mothers waking children from one bad dream.  Standing at the assembly line trying to keep a leg up above the fray, where does life go as it flows?

This is limber limbo.
This torn sail.
This scheme-seamed shanty.

This buffeted moon, ragged, gibbous,
gerrymandered.
This scar sequined by tear-light.
These skeletal ventricles.
This map.
I am lost in it . . .

Find myself in a language of romance remembering
rosaries under sky the Great Mother made in the wink of
an eye that lasted a million million years or more. The
stars above, beads of a broken rosary I restring with Santa
Marias in rifle-novenas. Under them, eagles released
from the gazes of dead American presidents, the green
fields of print. I have seen blood snaking down many legs
like any woman's blues, and blood spilled random from
mouths where kisses turn cold and give up spirits only
warm again inside children who multiply like alphabets
even the old ones learn to rearrange to meaning, who like
grains trouble the hot ash of murdered fields to rise again
in a miracle of loaves. I restring rosary beads of sweat and
blood stars, till something moves that I can stop in a fall-
en world held aloft by a Fate Mother whimsical and cal-
culating down to the trajectory of cells from minute to
minute to catastrophe everything aches in the legacy in
which I sit and fidget and figure the string
After a while
it's a knot /

        the seams of one string
        grown into another
        to tear when you go back
        to it to work it to the
        center / to work it loose
    here.
    you were the outsider.
    here.

you hid
what was too bright.
here
you were catered to.
here.
upheld.
here.
annihilated
the string winding
tighter and tighter
around the center
where you kept it
all together.
here is color.
here is hair.
here is sex.
here
desire.
here
despair.
here
grace.
here
deprival.
hubris, default, slight, and injury
begrudgment, debt, doubt,
insufficiency,
here.
rebuke.
here surprise.
here guilt and absolution.
here praise, now rage, here grit,
hypocrisy, envy, bravado,
self-abnegation, here loss, here grief,

here winds loneliness
persistent and long
all these little strings
of the Great Miss Thing

who sits and winds and winds and sings
until you can't find
whoever was inside
her endless yarns and boring tangles
and maybe as she would have it there is nothing
there and you are nowhere inside
her tumbled      meticulous pastime.


Sorrow can be a bland thing.  Or sorrow can be a bright
dream where I wake and loiter amid longing, long inside
myself, tenderhearted, quiescent and fine, new cobwebs
shining in morning omening decent weather.  Or song
flung up febrile, articulate outside word or thought, closed
and open for all who come after me.  What I remember
is yours to shape, relay, even what I cannot say but say.
Nothing breaks in or out of me, except now and then a
heart stretched too thin by rage.

Quartered at the crossroads,
                    what can you say
to Time,
Spite, Ruin,
Race, Sex,
Death, Class,
Loss, and Absence?
Trying to keep a leg up above the fray.

There are more than two sides
to your story; you have to watch

your back
for the tale you forgot.
Have to lift more than one leg
from each
pot of glue.
Then trying to keep your head up above the fray.
It ain't easy
to ease this discontent.
It ain't easy
at the intersection
where Eshu rules
to get a message through to Heaven
outside the extremities
of the world.

Trying to keep a leg up above the fray.
When lightning leaps down to stop me
I try
to hold and wreak electricity into my limbs.
God knows
I don't
know what I did to be so bruised.
Why can't I just be
in my glory?
in my mistakes?
in my dumb moves?
in my right?

                                        *


Make a cradle, a latticed lullaby, wily melody.
Open, extend labyrinthine memory.
Build with horizon seams
Anansi's elusive legacy.

Reconcile the paths     out and in.
They all lead to Africa again.
listening to what sisters say
trying to keep a leg up above the fray
gender, class, aristoi,
color,

dark dexterity,
loud luck spun out of your belly,
insouciant ochre gestures she cannot language,
increments of your lightsome gyres and swings,
all your dusky dance
your sepia entanglements she cannot unturn

She wants the God who loves you
to love her better.
She wants what you want.
She wants to move you out
of your mirror.
She wants you to watch her
in your mirror.

She wants what you want.
She wants to squat in the sun
of your cosmic design.
She wants you outlying solar
system to your self.

She wants to be you
at midnight.

You may keep your intelligent hair,
your natty dreads,
she doesn't want that

or want you to want it either.
But she wants your wise braid,
your sage threaded twists.
She wants your beauty to wear her name.
She wants to call your dance her dance.
She wants to explain you to you.
You may keep the lynch-tree memory in your dangerous
pendulum
You may keep quiet her part in it.
You may keep your retinue of furies.
You may keep the resume of bloodstains scattered in
the pattern of your turnings and return.
You may keep the shrunken heads of all your states.
You may keep famine and broken cobweb, houses of ill
repute.
You may keep assigned systems of least.
You may keep less and less.
You may keep
                crying.
You may keep clemency and charity.
She wants what's best for you.
She wants what you have:
dark dexterity,
loud luck spun out of your belly,
insoucient ochre gestures she cannot language,
increments of your lightsome gyres and swings,
all your dusky dance,
your sepia entanglements she cannot unturn.

                              *


How to express the cosmic emptiness:
Loneliness which has no form, seeks it,
So form may die as forms do and loneliness with it?

How to express the cosmic completion:
Black joy that brims preprimal light, cup overflowing
and ever replenished?

How to draw the two-faced energy of the heart
Of things—equal and opposite, touching in one


Body?  Touching then and knowing

God has seven electric curving
legs, and one extra, glowing radius; is archings, channels,
elegant, fire currents for bottom and abdomen.
God is greedy and satiated.  Prowling stars and under rocks.
Everything is alive and humming
Inside.  Nothing is lost.  Everything is
Swallowed:
All fallen
Hearts in the Heart of Things
are caught and kept
within themselves.

And then and now
a stumble.
Sometimes a walk is a tangle
A journey is a trip over yourself;
a stumble, a baggage
is all you are,
how far you go.
All the time—obstacle;
(future, past, present)
your body set back
a clock, fast, and slow

haywire hands scrambling across dumbfounded face.
A tangle of time.
Each step a mistake;
you are all the forks
in the roads you didn't
take.  Looped back.

Each prong a manifold longing.
Longing.  You jab the dust.
And say this is just my luck.
Just.

Any state I'm in is my statement.
Do not forget
me
shy to expose, closed
and expanding,
spanning, windows, doors, and gateways.

Do not forget
me.
Traveling.
These are my tracks.
Those chain-gang sweat-hours
I
grunted and hollered
when I laid every thing
down
and kept telling myself
after every line was laid
I could go somewhere.
I made a way where there was no way.
By the sweat of my belly.
I have to remember

how
I sang
how
it saved me

how to remember
lest I forget forever
and be lost in it.

Remember. Joy
this.
Dancing girl.
Double-dutch dream.
Spidergirl.
Okay.  Lace
on avenue.
Clotheslines. Catch.
The city spectral
in strokes of rhythm.
You.
Jumping through
dusk over sunset
on the line Mama threw
to catch the sun,
heat and scent
to nourish her.
You.
All.
Now. Loop the rope
across the moon.
Pull it.
Into your bed.
Let the shadows
know a him
a you.
A smile between two

faces.
Okay.
Spidergirl.
Joy.

You have the right to employ your wiles
while holding yourself tender like a child.

At last to slip the evil myths / elude the lies / let go
deceitful clothes. / To move then through a matrix
of legs / a midnight ramble / mossy stones rolling
all over a bed / translucent / to see through / circled
in sweat / crying in curve / cured / thighs and arms
akimbo / wide / bent / in labors / sweet / to work by
lamplight / to breath darkness threaded / by moonlight.
To stitch / in time / and save all there is / stitch long
then short and quick / zigzagging stitch / stitching /
what comes apart / what cleaves / and leaves and
cleaves / To forget what / we are making / simply sew
and sew and sew and sew / swearing at / all thumbs
mistakes / omnidextrous grace / sweating to finish
before dark grows too old to hold us / in.

Then
do remember me.
What I feel is mine!
What I think is mine!
What I work for is mine!
What Heaven gave me is mine
to give.

So I give life a spin and a weave.
I change
things.
The Joke is on me.

The Wit and the Will.
Whatever I get I give it a spin
then all is saved and kept within.

Watch the legs exquisite lift.
Quick craft. Arachnid Africanesque.
Warbleless walk the tightrope.
Watch the eyes myriad flash. Wise
open eye     without one lie
without or within.
The mouth a cradle of silk.
Silk in the mouth for my own.
Honestly.
I do not connive
only strive to be good.
If good is possible to be
and survive.
Purely.
Left to my own devices.
A generous decency would prevail.
Sensitive to the intricacies of each inside thing.
How would I judge myself or anyone who did not strive
to injure me or someone else?
I know this:
who can condemn the longing  of each inside thing
to be loved?
who can condemn me
because I did not inside
follow the rule of thumb?
I have the right to be loved once or twice in this life.
To be thought clever and sweet.
To have my needs gathered into one place to kiss.
I have the right to be loved once or twice.
Love, I have found, has no bias.

It stretches out of you
and makes itself known.
It does not seek to snare.
Yet
Leaves itself open
to entry.
There is no intrigue.
But injury still to be entered and left
longing.
When the world was tight with hope.
I become unstrung.
Like an instrument played wrong
who hates to hear its own music.
It is the music of what was not
meant to be.

\*

This is woman's work.  It is never done.
Always making something:  fan, canoe, kitchenette
apartment, church, silver-leaf on night's tree,
my end ambiguous as an inkblot test:
What I make out of me and air
is whatever you see shivering there,
or breathing, or waiting.
This is my work.  I am never done with my earthly art.
The end justifies the dream.
The dream is what seems.
Fingerprints made of moonlight.
Thin membranes etching, perhaps, a heart.

At first a stirring in extremities
where the world aches against me.
Emptily.

Or is it first a common nudge
in the city of the center?
Dim
citizens seeking franchise, substance?
Babies begging threads of milk?
Ambitious
ancestors asking form?
Or
Love longing host?

No matter or
all of these.

This matters:
what I made,
took Time and taught it a thing
or thought I did, or a part of me did.
Just this:  studious bits of life,
obedient, lucent

as a prayer,
a quelling of complaint,
a momentary ownership.
I lay down arms and rest in this—

a cradle,
a latticed lullaby in a blue palace of sky
down by a riverside,

on a tree
hangs a robe
once
dipped in deep
water, now
streaming.

**Coda: The Spider's Mantra**

All the things I knew by heart have come
to pass.   Spread,    eagled,   and wind across
the sky.

Think of the Sun and memorize me.

      A radiant web      traps all life
           and frees it.

A luminous umbilical cord   feeds all life
             and frees it.

Think of the Sun and memorize me.
Burning eternal-center

Alive and weaving well.
Glorious in heaven
      and earth.

At last.

Think of the Sun. . . .

# Koko

*for Mrs. Koko Taylor*

Hearing suffer when you live
loud. But you can feel
like you blind but see everything
by the smokiest light. Even
the wig rared back on my head
be alive and talking back, when
I bite lightning and make
a bow. Ain no accidents. Not
even the one knocked Pops and
me and the men over the side
of the winding road. It was
raining and the road was alive
hanging over death like a woman
out a window hollerin. On
Maxwell Street or like we call it
JewTown when evrybody was
on the outside near the good stank
of pola' sausage and onions
sweating and cryin grease, you
lie'ta find the tailor in the back
room makin them suits with big
shoulders and a shine if
you want it to do like a good
man would in some heat. Outside
it would have been a blind man
standing on the corner but he
still see his own skin and use
a spoon to push the lightning

through the tear in his guts.
Wouldn't no thimble do for him
wouldn't no thimble suit him.

There are different kinds
of naked, if you can understand
what makes it funny is I get
up in the morning in real life and cook and
clean house like any woman but
then before morning I let the
growl out the pocket of my mouth
and she come out in a
holler be naked and long-legged
split the smoke room swoop
and fly up in somebody eye.
Used to be a time when a woman
didn't go around making such suits
for anybody to wear
she just stay home and sew. But
I take the spool and go upside a man's
head he know he been struck
by lightning. He start
to moan and cry askin for a miracle
please hit me again. But I cain't
hear from the stage of Highway 61
not the way I'm workin with no clothes on
but sweat and the truth in a spangled costume
trying to make this suit fit every
body's misery and be walking too.
And, oooh, in the corner somebody
could a been done shot Shame, and
nobody know she was missing til the morning
after my voice be done wore off.  Lightning

be shook out they wounds and the growl be back in my
pocket when I ask my husband Pops
what he want for breakfast.  And
if he got some socks or somethin
need a needle.

# The Dome Spider Makes Her Toilette in Preparation for an Assignation

When I had come of age and was eager to be known
and know that for which I was born,
that for which I'd waited to taste, hungered,
craved in my chromosomes,
I sent my scent throughout my dwelling place and beyond.
When you came you tore off a piece of my virginal dome,
all the places my scent went
went with you tightly rolled into a packet
you carried with you like a carton for a gourmet take-out
or the olfactory photograph of your intended bride,
who was I, who had waited, and perfumed my world for you
so that you could gather my alluring missive and keep it to make
you heady, and secret it
so none of me could lure another,
to forestall all possible rivals
and I would be meant for you
alone.
What I must do is inbred born, yet
this is new to me, a virgin, I am nervous,
pheremones spent, inexperienced, excited.
I have only heard of these matters by way of gene
therefore I do not know, yet I notice while waiting for your return
how you take your own sweet time, unhurried as any certain

suitor,
even while that smell of mine
drives you wilder but not more than you are wise.
It will take some doing.
Loving me.

Teaching me the lessons of your cells.
When we copulate, "banded black and yellow bodies,"
when we mate,
it lasts a sweetest time,
"three to six hours of continuous action."
Seduction. Embrace. Afterwards kisses.
The thought of such goings on,
what I do not yet know,
sits with me, quivering,
as my scent sits with you, quivering.
It is enough to keep our species alive in a grand slow drag.
It is enough to make such lust persist in perpetuity.
It is enough to spell it in a song and call it love worth
waiting for.

# Spider Divine (of the Cameroons)

*Carlene*

Delicately, the priest decodes my privileged speech. He listens with learned grace when I pace my self-loom song throughout the night. He will read my lucid spell by morning's light; he reads like the lines on a palm. I am soothsayer, witch-spider, spider-wife, consultant against chaos and calamity, healer, hero, honored by heaven. Crying children with running sores, wombless women and blind men hainted, harassed, horrified, fly to my husband-priest. In the night he cries to his god through my delicate body. His asking-instrument rides my back. I move restlessly in sleep. I dream signs; I travel, I turn, I wander a web of missives, discreet, scrutable to his eyes; wild, minute a whisker from the Great Beast of Creation. My husband reads me well and lovingly.

# Lust: African-American Woman Guild

I wrap my legs around him.
 We swaddle and sway.
     We swing and bring the rain.
          A festival in famine.
          A thunder in heaven.

We curl together.   Sex, breath,
and all.     Till I'm breathless.
Quivering.    Complete.

This is Love.    I sing.
A tangle you don't mind.
A hot knot.
Figure it out.     Anybody.
     Where do he begin and I
          end?

# The Trick Is Not to Think:
# On the Art of Ballooning

*for DFaye*

The trick is not to *think*.
It's in the body (some light you let go—
then ride).

The trick is not to think.
Could it be the heart can breathe and drag you on its breath
as far as love can go?
Could it be the heart can breathe?
Don't think.

Could it be you could hold the heart's breath?
Don't think.
Could it be you could let the heart's breath go—
then follow?  Oh!  grabbing, grabbing hold.  Whatever is
traveling,
surging away!

Could it be you could cast off in blue sky
over blue water
and come upon a ship far at sea
you are at sea
but you be anyway?

Could it be you arrive far afield.  Gleefully.
            In a cradle.
            In your own backyard.
Could it be life took you for a ride?

Could it be you let your conscience be
                              your guide?

Or not.  (Just the heart.)
And wind up where you are.
The trick is not to think up scenes you've left behind.
Not to hold what stays
down.
Just leap out on a dream, an air of savoir faire
that leaps from inside you
and carries you, wondrous, bouyant,
to the place you are you     anew, oh! traveler,
traveling magic show
let go all old sorrow
away, away we go!

# The Skater

I'm up in the air
and I know it
this time . . .
                hangin by a thread
                        and I show my expertise
                        to fling and swing
                        like a cool skater
                        in icelike skirts.

I never was a social butterfly.
Just a small arachnee.
In a big weave.
My tortures tiny.
I won't complain.
I heard it on the radio.
The gospel singer sounded
like a voice from heaven
falling through anguish
into victory.
What could I say?
My limbs still tremble
and I pour my own rain
of swings.
How could I be so dumb
to cry in the middle of the night?
To shake my leg at Heaven
higher than the radio.
I felt like a fool.
Not to have seen
my own dim script on the wall.

Writing
Glory.
Glory.
Glory Be.

# Blessing

I

bless you with this kiss, silken, silver.
Wind your destiny in mine.  Dance down dark legs,
a many thousand wise.

In the middle of the road
a dark woman wears red.  She waves at you.
Throws kisses that sting and hold you to her.
You can taste her kisses all over you.  Now and again.

You will never forget.
You will never forget.

# Happily Ever After

I fell in love
and my self flew up
my eyes were two-way
mirrors
drowsy and alive
spying and direct
almost blunt
the truth
battering like a  heavy wind
but lifting lifting more
higher
I've been places in this love
traveled to the edges and insides
of my body.
Oh, what can I tell you?
You say it was nothing.
All in my mind.
Now the world is here
and I dream
like nobody's business.
Wide.  To imagine me.
And how thick is bliss.
And thin the ropes
that hold it here.
Even after. Tighter.
This Liberty.

# Peace, Be Still

Be still, I say.    And every bone, wing and
eye of earth is quiet.        I turn it on my stinging
laughter.    My keening joy.

Be river, I say,  and everything flows through
me in swift, flowing change.        I take my Time
and sip from it till it is all mine.            This earth,
bone, wing, and eye.        All rocks anciently
in my tight belly.
And I close my multitudinous eyes.
And I sleep.